Lives and Times

Benjamin Franklin

Jennifer Blizin Gillis

Heinemann Library
Chicago, Illinois

© 2004 Heinemann Library
a division of Reed Elsevier Inc.
Chicago, Illinois

Customer Service 888-454-2279
Visit our website at www.heinemannlibrary.com

Page layout by Cherylyn Bredemann
Photo research by Julie Laffin

Printed and bound in China by South China Printing Co Ltd

08
10 9 8 7 6 5 4 3

**Library of Congress
Cataloging-in-Publication Data**
Benjamin Franklin / Jennifer Blizin Gillis.
ISBN 1-4034-5324-1 (HC), 1-4034-5332-2 (Pbk.)
ISBN 978 - 1-4034-5324-2 (HC)
ISBN 978 - 1-4034-5332-7 (Pbk.)
The Cataloging-in-Publication Data for this title is on file with the Library of Congress.

Acknowledgments
The author and publishers are grateful to the following for permission to reproduce copyright material: Title page, p. 25 National Archives and Records Administration; icons, pp. 6, 10, 18, 22, 26, 24 Bettmann/Corbis; p. 4 Joseph Sohm/Visions of America/Corbis; p. 5 Dave G. Houser/Corbis; p. 7 Mary Evans Picture Library; pp. 8, 19 The Granger Collection, New York; pp. 9, 14, 16, 26, 29 Culver Pictures, Inc.; p. 11 Jerry Millevoi; p. 12 Gianni Dagli Orti/Corbis; p. 13 Historical Picture Archive/Corbis; p. 15 Liberty Bell Museum; p. 17 American Philosophical Society; pp. 20, 27 North Wind Picture Archives; p. 21 From the Collections of the University of Pennsylvania Archives; p. 28 Corbis

Cover Photograph by (top left) Bettmann/Corbis, (bottom left) The Corcoran Gallery of Art/Corbis, (bottom right) Culver Pictures, Inc.

The publisher would like to thank Charly Rimsa for her comments in the preparation of this book.

Every effort has been made to contact copyright holders of any material reproduced in this book. Any omissions will be rectified in subsequent printings if notice is given to the publisher.

Some words are shown in bold, **like this.** You can find out what they mean by looking in the glossary.

Contents

A Great American

Benjamin Franklin was a famous person in his own time. He is still famous today. He was a writer, a thinker, a scientist, a **diplomat,** and a great American.

The $100 bill has a picture of Benjamin Franklin on one side.

There are statues of Benjamin Franklin in many cities.

Some of our **rights** come from Benjamin's ideas about **government.** Some of the things we say come from Benjamin's writings. And we still use some of Benjamin's inventions.

Childhood

Benjamin was born in Boston, Massachusetts, in 1706. He had sixteen brothers and sisters. Benjamin's father made candles and soap for a living.

When Benjamin Franklin was born, Boston was the largest city in the thirteen American **colonies.**

Benjamin grew up in this house on Milk Street in Boston.

As a child Benjamin liked being outside. He liked to swim. He liked to read, too. Benjamin's father wanted him to become a **minister.**

Work

When he was twelve years old, Benjamin had to leave school and go to work. His older brother James was a printer. Benjamin became his **apprentice.** They printed a newspaper in the shop.

Printers set pieces of **type** in cases like the one on the right side of this picture.

Benjamin and James printed their newspaper on a press like this.

Soon, Benjamin began writing stories for the newspaper. But when Benjamin was seventeen years old, he and James argued. Then, Benjamin ran away to Philadelphia, Pennsylvania.

9

Life in Philadelphia

Benjamin found work as a printer. He lived in a **boarding house** next to the printing shop. The owner's daughter was named Deborah Read. Benjamin and Deborah became friends.

When Benjamin was a teenager, Philadelphia was a busy, exciting city.

In Philadelphia Benjamin met the governor of Pennsylvania. Governor Keith wanted Benjamin to start his own printing shop. He promised to give Benjamin money to go to London to buy a printing press.

Governor Keith's house is still standing in Pennsylvania.

Time in London

In the 1700s London was one of the busiest cities in the world. There were hundreds of printing shops there.

Benjamin sailed to London in 1724. Governor Keith said that he would make sure Benjamin got money when he arrived in London. But this did not happen. Benjamin had to start working.

Benjamin found a job in London with a printer. He liked to stay fit. He carried heavy trays of **type** up and down stairs. He also swam to stay in shape. Benjamin's friends thought this was strange!

Benjamin often swam in the Thames River in London. In the 1700s people thought getting too wet could make a person sick.

Success in Philadelphia

Benjamin went back to Philadelphia in 1726. He went back to his old printing job. He also started a club for young men. They met to talk about ideas. The club helped Benjamin start important projects.

Later in his life, Benjamin used many ideas from his club to help the city of Philadelphia.

Benjamin wrote stories for and printed this newspaper. It quickly became the most popular newspaper in Philadelphia.

First Newspaper Edited by Dr. Franklin.

Numb. XL.

THE
Pennsylvania GAZETTE.

Containing the freshest Advices Foreign and Domestick.

From Thursday, September 25. to Thursday, October 2. 1729.

Advertisements.

Benjamin decided to leave his job and start his own printing shop. He later took over a newspaper. It was called *The Pennsylvania Gazette.*

Marriage

Benjamin and Deborah Read were still good friends. In 1730 they were married.

This drawing shows Benjamin and Deborah on their wedding day.

Benjamin called Deborah his cheerful helper.

Deborah was Benjamin's partner. She helped him with his business. When Benjamin was away, Deborah kept the business going.

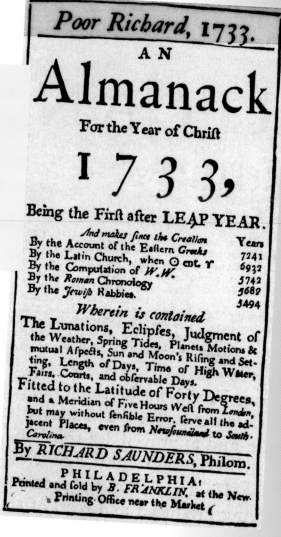

Printer Franklin

Benjamin's printing business was very good. He started a bookstore, too. In 1732 Benjamin wrote a book called *Poor Richard's Almanack*.

In the 1700s there were no weather reports like those on television today. People used **almanacs** to find out what the weather was going to be like.

Poor Richard, 1733.

AN

Almanack

For the Year of Christ

1733,

Being the First after LEAP YEAR.

And makes since the Creation — Years
By the Account of the Eastern Greeks — 7241
By the Latin Church, when ☉ ent. ♈ — 6932
By the Computation of W.W. — 5742
By the Roman Chronology — 5682
By the Jewish Rabbies. — 5494

Wherein is contained

The Lunations, Eclipses, Judgment of the Weather, Spring Tides, Planets Motions & mutual Aspects, Sun and Moon's Rising and Setting, Length of Days, Time of High Water, Fairs, Courts, and observable Days. Fitted to the Latitude of Forty Degrees, and a Meridian of Five Hours West from London, but may without sensible Error, serve all the adjacent Places, even from Newfoundland to South. Carolina

By RICHARD SAUNDERS, Philom.

PHILADELPHIA: Printed and sold by B. FRANKLIN, at the New. Printing-Office near the Market

This drawing shows some of Benjamin's wise sayings.

Benjamin's almanac had helpful information about weather, planting, and health. Benjamin wrote it under the name Richard Saunders. People loved the wise sayings and funny stories in the almanac.

Public Servant

In 1737 Benjamin became a **postmaster** for Philadelphia. He made many changes in the way mail was delivered. He improved roads and put up signs that made it easier for mail to get delivered.

By the time Benjamin was 40 years old, he was very successful.

Now, Benjamin began to think about how to help Philadelphia. He started a police force. He started a school, too. Today, that school is the University of Pennsylvania.

This is the seal of the University of Pennsylvania. It shows that the school was started in 1782.

Scientist and Inventor

When Benjamin was 42 years old, he sold his printing shop and bookstore. He started to **experiment** with electricity and lightning. He invented lightning rods to keep houses safe in thunderstorms.

Lightning rods are long pieces of metal on the roofs of houses. Lightning strikes the metal rod, not the house.

Bifocal glasses let people see better close up and far away without having to change glasses.

Benjamin invented many helpful things. He invented a street lamp that gave out more light. He invented a pole that helped people reach things in high places. He also invented a new kind of glasses.

War

The Second Continental Congress was an important meeting in Philadelphia. People met to plan a new government for the thirteen colonies.

In 1775 the **Revolutionary War** began. Benjamin wanted to help his country. The people of Pennsylvania asked him to speak for them at the Second Continental Congress.

Benjamin wanted all thirteen **colonies** to come together under one **government.** Some of his ideas later became part of the **Constitution** of the United States.

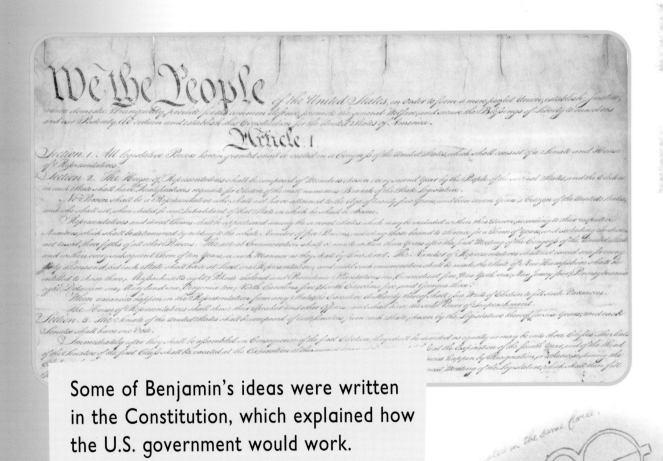

Some of Benjamin's ideas were written in the Constitution, which explained how the U.S. government would work.

Speaking for America

People liked Benjamin's ideas. They asked him to help write the **Declaration of Independence. Congress** asked him to go to France to get help with the **Revolutionary War.**

While he was in France, Benjamin liked to dress like someone from the American West. He wore a hat made from raccoon fur.

This picture shows a group of French ladies making a fuss over Benjamin.

Benjamin stayed in France for about nine years. He got French leaders to send money and soldiers to America. When the war ended, Benjamin was asked to help write the **peace treaty.**

Speaking Out Against Slavery

Benjamin sailed back to Philadelphia in 1785. He was almost 80 years old and very sick. But he was more popular than ever! The people of Pennsylvania asked him to be governor.

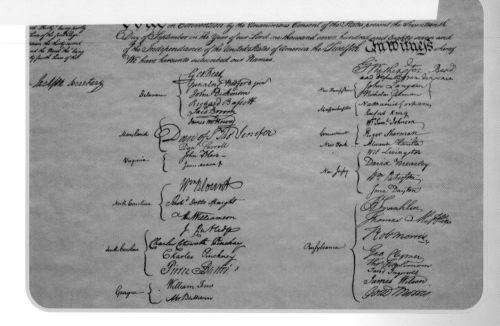

Benjamin was Pennsylvania's governor when he signed the Constitution of the United States in 1787.

Epitaph written 1728.

The Body of
B Franklin Printer,
(Like the Cover of an old Book
Its Contents torn out
And stript of its Lettering & Gilding)
Lies here, Food for Worms.
But the Work shall not be lost;
For it will, (as he believ'd) appear once more,
In a new and more elegant Edition
Revised and corrected,
By the Author.

Benjamin was not happy with one thing about the **Constitution.** It let people in some of the new states own **slaves.** He began writing and speaking out against this. Benjamin died in 1790.

Fact File

- Benjamin sailed across the Atlantic Ocean many times during his life. This was very unusual in the 1700s.
- Benjamin wrote an **autobiography.**
- Books were very expensive, so Benjamin started the first library in the United States. People could borrow books from the library instead of buying them.
- Benjamin had the **Gulf Stream** added to maps of the Atlantic Ocean to help sea captains get to the United States from Great Britain more quickly.
- Benjamin printed a *Poor Richard's* **Almanack** every year for 25 years.

Timeline

1706	Benjamin Franklin is born on January 17.
1718	Benjamin becomes an **apprentice** in James Franklin's printing shop.
1723	Benjamin runs away to Philadelphia.
1724	Benjamin goes to London.
1726	Benjamin returns to Philadelphia.
1729	Benjamin begins *The Pennsylvania Gazette.*
1730	Benjamin marries Deborah Read.
1732	Benjamin publishes the first *Poor Richard's Almanack.*
1748	Benjamin retires from business at age 42.
1774	Deborah dies.
1775	The **Revolutionary War** begins.
1776	Benjamin goes to France.
1785	Benjamin returns to Philadelphia.
1790	Benjamin dies on April 17.

Glossary

almanac   book that predicts what the weather will be like in the coming year and that also contains other useful facts. An old way to spell it is "almanack."

apprentice   person who works for someone in order to learn a certain job

autobiography   book someone writes about their own life

boarding house   house where people pay for a room to live and food to eat

colony   group of people who live in a new land but are governed by people from their old country

Congress   group of men and women who make the laws for the United States

Constitution   important paper that explains how the government works and the rights that people have in the United States

Declaration of Independence   important paper that was written to tell the government of Great Britain that the thirteen American colonies were free

diplomat   person who does things to help people in their state or country

experiment   to test or prove something

government   group of people who rule a country

Gulf Stream   part of the Atlantic Ocean where the water is warmer than the rest of the ocean

minister   person who leads a church

peace treaty   paper that explains how countries will behave toward each other after they have been at war

postmaster   person in charge of making sure mail is delivered in a town or country

Revolutionary War   war that the thirteen American colonies fought against Great Britain so that they could be a separate country

right   something which all people deserve to have, like freedom

slave   person who is owned by another person, and who has to do work for the other person

type   metal letters that were used to print things in the days before computers

More Books to Read

Abraham, Phillip. *Benjamin Franklin*. New York: Scholastic, 2002.

Rustad, Martha. *Benjamin Franklin*. Mankato, Minn.: Capstone Press, 2002.

An older reader can help you with these books:

Gregson, Susan R. *Benjamin Franklin*. Mankato, Minn.: Bridgestone Books, 2001.

Roop, Connie and Peter Roop. *In Their Own Words: Benjamin Franklin*. New York: Scholastic, 2000.

Index